What People A

"Carla's book is a game c
purpose and creativity."

— Tammy Kling, CEO OnFireBooks

"Dr. Carla is a true American success story; her whose analysis of Walt Disney and some of his magic will give you a glimpse into how she has created the perfect life for herself and her family, which you can do too."

— Michael Casey, international speaker, author of *The Billion-Dollar Idea,* product developer, and founder of 8dates.

"I've known Carla for over a decade. She has made quantum leaps in every aspect of her life and has taken this wisdom and written it around the magical thinking of Walt Disney. I could not put her book down due to her storytelling and the powerful way she explains the complex subject of quantum physics and how we can utilize this 'magic' to create the life of our dreams.

"As Cinderella is quoted in the book, 'The greatest risk you will ever take is to be seen as you are.' Take the risk and read this book; however, be prepared to take your own magic carpet ride, because you will discover how powerful you truly are."

— Pam Sowder, CNO and cofounder of Itworks International.

"This book will change the definition of imagination and will impact lives for a thousand generations."

— Tiarra Tompkins, CEO OnFireBooks

"I would say the *biggest* 'ah-ha' I had reading after reading *What Walt Knew* and joining Carla on the Mastermind Cruise was writing out my dream life/day. It allowed me to realize that I was worthy of more than just being complacent and gave me permission to level up. Within six weeks, we moved into our ideal neighborhood/school system across state and God one hundred percent provided for all of it!"

— Ashley Mayfield, Tribal Leader

"I dare you to immerse your open mind into Dr. Burns's book *What Walt Knew.* If you do, I guarantee you will emerge with a new focus, perspective, and action plan to change the trajectory of your life. Do so, and get ready to live the life you dream!"

— Bruce Pulver., author, speaker, encourager, believer in the power of our words
Above The Chatter, Our Words Matter

"I usually have to work hard to start and finish a book; however, that was not the case with *What Walt Knew.* I loved it! I didn't want to put it down."

— Ryan Wells, Children's Cup

"We truly become what we think. I had no idea there was *real* science behind this. If you let negativity in, negativity will come out. I didn't understand all of the science, but I surely know that there is no space for anything but positivity about where I want go in my brain!"

— Amanda Pruitt, stay-at-home millionaire mom

After reading *What Walt Knew*, I joined Carla on the Imaginations Masterminds Disney Cruise. Working with Carla gave me excellent guidance and support, showing me how to use transformative thinking and imagination to reach my goals. The exercises of healing your inner child and being in a magical setting are a gift. Carla always reminds me of my faith! The experience was awesome, and you leave the adventure with a crystal-clear vision for your life purpose and business.

— Michelle Lersch, realtor

"Going on the Disney Dream and being able to learn from a leader like Carla Burns changed my mindset forever. At the time, I had picked up a book on the millionaire mindset, and I felt that because I was in the presence of top income earners, I had to step up my own game. Being on the cruise and getting to know her on a personal level made me realize I was no different. Yes, the others had a few more commas and zeros in their paychecks than I did, but that's because they had a urgency to get there—an urgency that I was just discovering because I was a new mom with a newborn the first time I went on the cruise.

"Since the cruise, Carla has become my mentor. She's always been so open with me, and I have learned a lot just by watching and listening. She leads by inspired action, and that's the way I wanted to lead my team. Just a few months after the Imagination Master Cruise, I am so happy to report I got a *huge* promotion, a promotion I was working on for *years*. I broke through a big glass ceiling! I fell short many times, and I was close for months. But that last little push that happened in was the result of a complete shift of mindset. I journaled, and I read Carla's book *What Walt Knew*. The four keys 🔑 kept me going; even in moments when I felt defeated, I would open that book and read some more. Going forward in my business, I will always refer back to it because the wisdom is there, the roadmap is there. The concept of staying positive while facing adversity is so tough when you are going through it, but I felt that the four keys 🔑 kept my path and mindset clear; I couldn't have done it without that shift. Anything is possible if you just believe!"

— Mellisa, work-from-phone full-time mom

"Carla's influence and impact on my life has been tremendous. Because of her teachings, I am being more, doing more, believing more, expecting more, and truly stepping into who God called me to be. I am and will forever be grateful for her wisdom, her willingness to learn and share, and the products she has created to help us all grow."

— Denise Walsh, author of *Design Your Dream Life*

WHAT WALT KNEW

4 Keys to Unlock
the Unlimited Power of
IMAGINATION

Carla Burns, PhD

Clovercroft Publishing

What Walt Knew: 4 Keys to Unlock the Unlimited Power of
Your Imagination

Published by Clovercroft Publishing, Franklin, Tennessee
Senior Editor: Tammy Kling
Executive Editor: Tiarra Tompkins
Copy Edit by Adept Content Solutions

Cover Design by Nellie Oh

Interior Design by Adept Content Solutions

Printed in the United States of America

978-1-948484-62-6

Disclaimer
The ideas and concepts stated in *What Walt Knew* are based
on the personal experiences the author learned from reading
and following Walt Disney and do not represent the Walt
Disney brand.

CONTENTS

INTRODUCTION

Have you ever wondered why is it so easy for some to live a magical life while others struggle to even get through life? That very question kept me up at night. For the past several years I have been observing patterns and habits in people, including myself, to find the answer. This book is designed to share my personal insights and the wisdom I have gained from Walt Disney.

Walt Disney knew that there are four keys to unlock the unlimited power of your imagination that allow you to create your own magical life. These four keys, like many of the lessons I will share, are woven into Disney classic fairy tales. Some of the messages are hidden while others, like the four keys can be found in Walt's famous quote:

> *"First, think. Second, believe.*
> *Third, dream, and last, dare!"*

Your imagination is a powerful tool. Walt knew this. Has it ever crossed your mind that the Disney classics your parents read to you as a child that were supposed to put you to sleep, are actually meant to wake you up? Snow White, Cinderella, Sleeping Beauty, Aladdin, and my personal favorite—Peter Pan—are full of hidden messages. There is scientific, spiritual, and practical wisdom found in these childhood favorites that hold the key to create whatever you want in life. It is possible Walt chose specific tales to animate that would plant a seed of curiosity into your early childhood subconscious. Certainly, his plan was to share this wisdom in a childlike way so that it would become clear to us as adults when we could look at it from a different perspective. Walt was filled with childlike wonder, yet he was much more than a dreamer. He valued faith, family, and good fortune for all. Walt was a visionary and believed these foundational beliefs are at the core of the four ways you can live the life you dream of.

In 1949, Disney wrote in *Guideposts* magazine: "I believe firmly in the efficacy of religion, in its powerful influence on a person's whole life. It helps immeasurably to meet the storm and stress of life and keep you attuned to the divine inspiration. Without inspiration, we would perish. All I ask of myself, is 'Live a good Christian life.' To that objective I bend every effort in shaping my personal, domestic, and professional activities and growth."

Raised in a Christian home, I don't believe it is a coincidence that Walt chose specific fables to bring to life that would transfer his core values to the lives of listeners. You will discover, as I did, that there is a direct correlation between spirituality and Walt Disney's animated classic tales. Although these tales were written hundreds of years ago, the wisdom is timeless. Today with a fresh perspective you will also see that there is spiritual truth and practical wisdom that is backed by new science.

The Science of Quantum Physics!

For over ten years I have studied quantum physics and neuroscience. In the beginning I studied these to help break through my own limitations, only to discover how fascinating the possibilities of the mind are. Since then I have become obsessed with helping people like you understand the correlation between spirituality and science to realize their own success. Success has always been easy for me, so it bothered me when thousands of people I coach would wonder, "Why you and not me?" I did not come from a wealthy background. Both of my parents worked hard and saved to provide my brother and me with all we needed, but I was not living like the princess I believed I am. In fact, I was born and raised in a small Canadian fishing village without a castle to be found. There was really not a lot of inspiration or models of success that I could follow. I am not the only success story that came from humble beginnings. I did not have anything on the outside that made me different; I had something on the inside I learned from Walt Disney. For years I couldn't explain my supernatural success. Today, after completing my PhD I realized I now have the language to explain what it was. The secret is that the four keys unlock something magical on the inside. I have used these four keys to create my own magical life, and I'm certain that anyone can create success, including you!

The first key I applied to my own life was the powerful connection of science and spirituality. It is called IMAGINATION. Using my imagination sparked by Disney classics and applying spiritual principles, I learned that I could create anything my heart desired with focused thoughts. This ability to manifest my desires began around age six, during my most impressionable years. It was then I first experienced the magic of imagination and believing in fairy godmothers, pixie-dust, princesses, and the wonder of this life. I remember words like "forever more" and "happily ever after" were some of the first words I learned. As you read these pages, you will see clearly how the power of imagination is the connection of science and spirituality.

That Is What Walt Knew!

The Merriam-Webster dictionary defines *imagination* as follows: "the capacity to produce images, ideas, and sensations in the mind without any immediate input of the senses (such as seeing or hearing)."

When is the last time you intentionally used your mind and really paid attention to creating an idea without using any of your natural senses?

For example, when I wanted to write this book, I first imagined it already done. I knew what the cover would look like and all of the stories I would share before I wrote a single sentence. I would imagine seeing it on bookshelves in the airport shops. I travel often and can remember even speaking out loud to my family, "Look! There is my book." They would roll their eyes and laugh. You may get this reaction too as you begin to apply these keys to your own life. Don't let that stop you. I would dream about walking into the Disney dream cruise shops and seeing this book displayed for guests to purchase. I even talk about it being translated to other languages. Just out of curiosity, I wonder, where you purchased this copy you have in your hands? This book is one of several dreams I have used the four keys to manifest into my life.

When Is the Last Time You Had a Dream?

No doubt, if Walt were here, he would agree that when quantum physics and spiritual principles combine in understanding the deeper meaning of his classic tales, they can be a powerful guide to create the life you want. The evil stepmother, the princess searching for her prince, pixie dust, and magic carpets—all these stories are filled with hidden wisdom.

By the end of our journey you will understand how to think, believe, dream, and—if you dare—create your own magical life.

We will explore the idea that science and spirituality not only align but also explain how imagination works. Many of the concepts are based on knowledge found in ancient manuscripts as well as a new quantum view of our world and how it relates to manifesting your dreams. The portal to understanding the four keys is the retelling of some of my personal favorite Disney classics. With a quantum perspective I will reveal the hidden messages I have found that unlock the power of your imagination.

Faith, Trust, and Pixie Dust Will Take on a Whole New Meaning!

I have been successful in creating my own magical life using Walt's four keys and believe beyond a doubt that if you will believe, you can too!

1. What is the powerful connection between science and spirituality?

2. If you had a magic mirror to see your life 1 year from now what is one thing you would be doing?

3. What are the 4 things Walt knew were needed to create a magical life?

"A DREAM IS A WISH YOUR HEART MAKES"

My heart's desire is . . .

Fill this page with all the dreams you hold most dear in as much detail as possible. Don't hold back! Give yourself permission to imagine your pen has magic ink and that what you write on this page will be sprinkles with pixie dust.

It will be fun to look back after reading this book to see how your dreams expand don't worry you will have plenty of pages in the back to create new ones!

_____

_____

_____

_____

_____

_____

_____

_____

CHAPTER 1
WALT'S WISDOM

What if your life could have a happy ending? Walt wanted everyone to have a happily-ever-after ending. If you choose it and you train your mind to look at the world and circumstances with childlike faith, you begin to see wonder and magic in all circumstances. Walt's faith showed him the importance of seeing the world through the eyes of a child.

Growing up like most little girls, I dreamed of being a princess and played my role well with fancy dresses, dreaming of a prince and imagining I lived in a castle. Today those who know me refer to me as a princess in the best sense of this word. I love all things that sparkle and feel a strong desire to visit castles all over the world. If there is a chance to wear a ball gown, I am all in. My ability to think and act this way using imagination was cemented by Walt's books. I have gained priceless wisdom in his countless inspirational quotes. The classic tales Walt brought to life were the catalyst that have brought me to where I am today. I respectfully call him a mentor.

Although Einstein first said, "If you want your children to be intelligent, read them fairy tales." Walt knew this too. Two of the greatest visionaries of our time knew that imagination is the key to all knowledge. This awareness holds the key to create the life you dream of.

The wisdom Walt had in common with Einstein was light years ahead of its time. He knew something special, something magical, that captured the hearts of millions of people all over the world. He believed and lived this truth: all it takes is faith, trust, and a little pixie dust to live a magical life. With this mindset and the courage to act, Walt dared to prove that you can live the life of your dreams. The tales Walt chose to bring to life have deeper meaning and are filled with life lessons. Walt may not have known this, but many of the concepts also align with quantum physics. Walt claims to have been divinely inspired, and his magical thinking was well before his time. I often wonder if he was inspired by Einstein or if it is all coincidence? What about the original authors of the fables we have grown to cherish? What was the inspiration that sparked their imagination to bring us such timeless tales?

I don't believe there are coincidences in life. Do you?

Walt referred to a higher Truth in the world guiding him. Growing up in a faith-filled home, I imagine he was taught the teaching of Jesus regarding a kingdom within where God resides. Walt understood the true meaning of this "kingdom" was within. I'm convinced that when Walt created the Magic Kingdom, it was meant to represent that place in all of us, the kingdom called imagination. It is there, within you, that you are divinely inspired with visions and dreams. As a child it was at the Magic Kingdom that I could dream and felt most like a real-life princess. As an adult it's still where I go when I want to be inspired to dream big or need a little sprinkle of pixie dust.

Have you been to Magic Kingdom?

Everything about it is magical! If you have, do you remember your first experience walking down the street seeing Cinderella's castle in the background? It still brings out a feeling of wonder in me today. Something magical happens when you surround yourself with wonderful and creative things. I have stayed young at heart from frequent visits to the park and continue to visit frequently. Something happens to neurons in my brain the moment I drive through the gate; they start to fire in a new creative and positive way! There will be people in your life who think this is crazy or childish. Do you think Walt and Einstein cared when others called them crazy?

The Real Magic is Within Each of Us

No matter what age you are, you are never too old to have a dream. It's impossible not to feel a sense of childlike wonder when you enter the Magic Kingdom gates. Walt truly created a place of wonder and amazement, which is every child's dream to visit. What if you could access that same feeling every day in your own inner kingdom?

What Walt knew from being raised in a Christian home was that the kingdom Jesus spoke of in ancient manuscripts was literally within. Quantum science refers to this same kingdom as consciousness, where your imagination creates reality. I am going to refer to both consciousness and imagination throughout these pages; however, both are the same, depending on your world view. This is important to understand the keys as they all require a new way of thinking.

If you have been to the Magic Kingdom, what's your favorite attraction or ride?

One of my favorites is "It's a Small World." I was so sad to hear that it was a ride that was being discontinued. I'll bet you are singing those lyrics right now too. "It's a world of laughter a world of cheer . . ." Those of us who grew up knowing and loving Disney know every word to many of the songs. Why do you think that ride and that song have such an impact? For me it was a reminder that even though we come from different backgrounds, we are all connected in the kingdom.

Have you noticed how happy people there are?
Even Grumpy can't help but smile humming along.
Something else I noticed as I got older was that
all the characters from every country wore white
robes at the end of the ride. Walt was sharing the
eternal message of the possibility of unity on earth,
a vision of a world without judgment. How often do
you judge someone based on religion, skin color, or
nationality? When it comes to imagination, there is
a place for everyone to dream in the kingdom.

Have you given yourself permission to dream?

Visiting the castle year after year beginning
around age ten is where I gave myself permission to
dream. Dreaming doesn't stop just because we age.
Maybe you grew up like I did in a small town, not
going anywhere anytime soon. Sometimes the places
we live and the people around us can steal your
dream. Walt Disney's ideas were rejected. He was
told "no" many times. The unkind words people
say can make it seem as though your vision is too
farfetched. Walt stayed focused on his vision and
the dream he had to impact people on the deepest
level. We too have to look beyond what is around
us and persevere. I was from a very small fishing
town in Atlantic Canada with not much to see but
plenty to dream about. Thankfully my parents
brought us to Florida every year so that my brother
and I had opportunities to see what was beyond the
town limits. The Magic Kingdom was something
that we visited every year. I remember the year

I turned twelve. Little did I know on this yearly family Disney trip I would personally experience the creative power of imagination. I was not consciously aware of it, but this trip set the stage for my future me! It was the beginning of the story I had imagined for myself as a young girl listening to Cinderella. I remember my family stayed in Saint Petersburg, just down the road from a pink castle hotel, the Don Cesar! I could see it off in the distance and begged my parents to take me. That pink castle was where I belonged.

With great hesitation and much persuasion, my parents agreed to quickly walk me through. My parents were hard workers and provided more than most kids needed or could want; however, they held a mindset that we didn't belong in a place like that. These are the lies within all of us that Walt knew could be transformed by your imagination. The subconscious conditioning that we didn't belong was programmed within my parents' minds from their childhood experiences, but not mine. That idea was not sitting well with me! I had grown up believing I was a princess, and of course I should be in a place like that. It was practically my home! As a twelve-year-old girl I walked through that pink castle hotel, and I imagined myself there as a guest one day. I took every incredible image into my imagination. I remember the chandeliers and the marble and gold staircase. I smelled the aroma of the fresh-cut flowers and the sound of the waves crashing on the crystal sand beach. In those few moments I could see myself there and would continue to dream about it for years. When we dream with such vivid images, it creates a sense of understanding in the way the nonphysical world works. I knew that I belonged there. I fully expected to be back as a guest.

One day when I least expected it I made my return to that pink castle. I not only stayed there, I stayed in the penthouse, and ate at the chef's table. I won this experience as a top earner in my company and shared this memory as a testament that dreams do come true. Sometimes dreams will take forty days and some will take forty years, but if you will believe you are worthy and remain in faith that it is already done, it is.

Coincidence? No, remember I don't believe that. Nothing is random; we all can think, chose, and create. You are doing it every day at a subconscious level.

On that day I saw my dream of that castle in the distance, my twelve-year-old mind was hard at work standing in the lobby looking at the chandeliers and gold-trimmed frames, smelling the fresh cut flowers, and seeing the smiling faces of the guests. I consciously used my imagination and chose that for my future self. I wasn't thinking about how or when; I was only twelve years old, enjoying every second of this experience. Too often we forget to just enjoy life and have fun. Walt himself couldn't have imagined a more magical place and that the adventure of a lifetime was about to unfold. I knew in my heart I was a princess, and the wisdom I learned from Walt confirmed it.

Walt seemed to understand that there are laws that exist that govern the natural world we see. He also knew there are spiritual laws that form the supernatural world that we cannot see. Although the supernatural can't be seen, it is very real. This is the realm of consciousness where your imagination creates your reality. Quantum physics describes this as the field of possibilities. If Walt were alive, I'm convinced he would be the first to adopt a quantum world view. You see, imagination is supernatural, and can't be seen or explained, much like faith. Unseen spiritual laws are entangled in reality and play a critical part of the formula to create the life you were made for. Thanks to my faith and the wisdom gained from the life of Walt Disney, I have become an enthusiast of power and possibilities. I appreciate the gift of the mind, the place where imagination changes everything.

Walt knew imagination is a gift from God and where he put his trust.

"Anything is possible if we have faith, trust, and a little bit of pixie dust."

Walt was very open about his faith and his belief in a higher Truth. He used divine inspiration and valued this faith in God. I wonder what Walt knew about the mediator between God and man's mind.

Quantum theorists ask this same question. Who holds the key to the kingdom within? Who is the mind? No one really knows for sure. Much of Walt's wisdom was based on faith. Quantum physics theory is that there is a mediator to the divine called human consciousness. It is my personal belief that Walt referred to consciousness as your imagination. Both refer to the creative force in the universe. Both are within your own mind.

Individually faith, trust, and pixie dust all have an equally important role in creating our lives.

Faith—in Peter Pan's classic quote Walt showed us the importance of having faith as the first step in creating a magical life. Ancient manuscripts refer to faith as the end result of using your imagination to create something from nothing. When your creative consciousness is in alignment with a higher Truth, your heart's desires are created according to your faith. With a focused, unwavering mind, faith becomes the manifestation of supernatural ideas into the natural world.

Trust—is the ability to surrender what you think you need to control and allow the higher Truth Walt knew to be greater than yourself to prevail. Trust is resting in the space of unknowns, being unattached to the outcome yet expecting something incredible. This is also the quantum law of nonresistance, letting go and allowing God. Trusting in something you can't see is risky but it is also a choice.

Pixie Dust is light energy. Photons! The infinitely endless particles of creative energy we find in quantum space that form and hold everything together. This subatomic power is what forms what you can see and touch from your creative consciousness. This light energy is at work in us and through us and begins at the moment of conception. What Walt knew is that the light that has always been with you is critical to manifesting what you see on earth.

These three things—faith, trust, and pixie dust are the foundation to understanding how Walt's four keys will unlock the power of your imagination.

Once you know, there is no turning back. I will give you the keys if you are ready. Now turn the page and open the door to your unlimited power.

1. Have you giving yourself permission to dream? If not why not?

2. What have you known to be true and your heart but have not trusted?

3. What or who have you judged that no longer serves you?

4. What is one belief you held that you can apply the law of faith to?

5. What does the kingdom within mean to you?

CHAPTER 2
FIRST, THINK!

"I think of a child's mind as a blank book.
During the first years of his life, much will
be written on the pages. The quality of that
writing will affect his life profoundly."
—Walt Disney

Thoughts are the foundation of your reality! Walt knew the power to create a magical life begins with thoughts, yet some of you pay no attention to your daily thoughts. Walt also knew that thoughts have the ability to turn themselves into magical things. It's your own level of mastery of thinking habits that determine your level of success in this life.

Key #1 If you want to master a magical life, you must first master your mind.

Can you name one thing that exists that was first not created by someone's imagination?

What if I told you that everything you know to be true first began within your imagination? You first had to THINK it. This very planet and the air you breathe originated with a thought. How did you arrive here at this moment with this book in your hands? You thought of it! Something deep, deep inside you wants answers to the hard questions. You were searching and have found exactly what you needed at this exact moment in time. There are no coincidences; only choices. It's not a coincidence that successful people make thinking successful ideas a priority. Now that I am aware of the power thoughts have, I pay very close attention to any negative thoughts that pop up. I have disciplined myself to keep my attention focused on what I want.

Walt knew that right now there is a force bigger than you and I directing your very steps. There is! It's your gift God gave you called the mind, and from it flows the creative power of imagination. We all have a mind and yet few understand how to use it for the highest good. To really grasp what I am going to share in these pages, there is one truth that you must become intimately aware of.

You are the sole creator of your reality, never a victim. You are consciousness, a divinely created spirit of creative energy in a human body. What makes humans totally unique is we are the only created beings that have the ability to think and direct energy using our thoughts. I have found what is hard to accept about this statement is the accountability of this power. If you find yourself in a prison of negative thinking, it is you that put yourself there. Only you that can set yourself free. Do you think Walt Disney could have created the legacy he did with powerless thinking?

> *"All the adversity I've had in my life, all my troubles and obstacles, have strengthened me . . . You may not realize it when it happens, but a kick in the teeth may be the best thing in the world for you."*
> —Walt Disney

This is the point where you may want to grab a cup of tea and settle in. You may resist what I am going to share in the beginning but read on if you are ready to wake up to your highest good.

It's not your circumstances that make you who you are; it's your thoughts. It all starts within your mind. This is not a new idea, although it may be the first time anyone has told you. The ancient prophets also knew the power of thoughts. They knew what is seen is not made out of things that are visible. Two thousand years ago, they did not have our high-powered microscopes yet they knew that thoughts create. Today we have the evidence, discovered by quantum pioneer Max Planck in his famous observer experiment. In this experiment Planck showed that by simply applying focused attention, particles behaved in a certain way. When there was no one watching nothing happened. How can this be?

Quantum concepts are not just science; they are a worldview that can explain love, life, and even death based on the power of your thoughts. This is a radical way to think that takes adult responsibility combined with childlike faith. Walt knew that it takes a powerful shift in thinking if you want to create a magical life.

I understand that foreign concepts like quantum physics, neuroscience, and even spirituality can be intimidating and honestly self-interpreted. To understand anything new, it's important to have an open mind and childlike wonder. Become curious. As a child you came into this world fearless without negative thinking. Walt knew the early years of your life were programmed. Any thinking outside of limitless is something you learned and must be transformed.

If you are like the average person, your thoughts are negative, repetitive, and limiting. To create the life you want this type of thinking has to change. It is a foundational practice found in Disney classics that you must be willing to learn how to think magically. Magic carpets, fairy god mothers, and sprinkles of pixie dust require you to think back to when you were a child. What thoughts filled your mind? It's no secret that I am a huge Walt Disney follower. There is something very magical woven into the backdrop of his popular childhood stories that helped me in my own journey. Growing up listening to Disney classics allowed me see the world with wonder and happy endings. Although Walt did not write these stories himself, through my research I can see that Walt had a similar insight about these classic tales.

Let's dive in and think back to your childhood favorite!

Memories from your childhood favorites will allow us to go back to a time when you were impressionable. I will be using words like quantum, consciousness and neuroscience that are concepts most children have never thought about. It may seem overwhelming, but if you read this with the eyes and ears of a child, it will help you understand. Be open to the spiritual lessons and quantum principals in a way that brings out your childlike curiosity without judgment of all you already know. These limiting beliefs you were taught as a child need to be looked at in a new light.

For example, as a child I was taught that the parable of the kingdom was a place. I thought that in order to enter you must become like a little child. If you are familiar with this teaching of Jesus, where do you think the kingdom is? This is the same kingdom I spoke of in the previous chapter. I grew up believing that it was a place in the clouds with no adults allowed and that we magically transformed back to age seven when we died. Walt knew the kingdom was your imagination. Both could be considered ridiculous, but I had never understood what Jesus meant by saying "The kingdom is within" until the day when as an adult, with a quantum view, I understood that Jesus was referring to your creative consciousness. When you chose to think, you create. This is using your free will, the will to choose. I once thought that free will meant one choice, heaven or hell. This is the type of limited thinking you will need to transform. Each day you will have many opportunities to use your free will to choose what thoughts you want to create. Old limiting beliefs will no longer serve you and the life you really want. This type of thinking needs to be replaced with truth and new ideas to make a quantum leap.

What other things did you think of as a child that sound silly today as an adult? Never underestimate the power of your thoughts. Take every thought captive.

Do you have fears? I don't know many adults that can honestly say they are not fearful of something. When you were a child, you weren't afraid to jump on the bed, learn new things, and be bold. Children have a unique ability to imagine and create the grandest adventures without ever leaving the backyard. Fear is not a concept learned until later in life.

One of our greatest philosophers of ancient times, Aristotle, knew exactly what Walt and Einstein understood. The first years of childhood are the most critical time in forming our thinking habits.

> *"Give me the boy at age seven and*
> *I will show you the man."*
>
> —Aristotle

A modern-day philosopher, Dr. Bruce Lipton, explains this famous quote and the origin of these patterns in his book *Biology of Belief* as follows:

Between two and six years of age, the child's brain activity ramps up and operates primarily in the range of theta. While in the theta state, children spend much of their time mixing the imaginary world with the real world.

The predominant delta and theta activity expressed by children younger than six signifies that their brains are operating at levels below consciousness. Delta and theta brain frequencies define a brain state known as a hypnagogic trance—the same neural state that hypnotherapists use to directly download new behaviors into the subconscious minds of their clients.

In other words, the first six years of a child's life are spent in a hypnotic trance!

A child's perceptions of the world are directly downloaded into the subconscious during this time, without discrimination and without filters of the analytical self-conscious mind, which doesn't fully exist. No negative self-talk, no boundaries of imagination. Consequently, our fundamental perceptions about life and our role in it are learned without our having the capacity to choose or reject those beliefs. We were simply programmed.—

Do you have fond memories of your early childhood? Can you see how those years have made an impact on the life you are living today?

Memories from your childhood will allow us to go back to a time when you were impressionable. You are going to remember how to use your imagination. It is still there; you use it every day. The creative part is just dormant from day to day life and the impression of how we are supposed to think in this world as grownups. Walt knew the power of thinking magically is directly tied to the ability to think like a child. Walt knew that the real trouble with the world was too many people grow up.

Many of you have been sleepwalking through life. You grew up and forgot the magic of who you really are. Just like Sleeping Beauty had to wake up to receive her royal destiny and live happily ever after, it's time for you to wake up to your highest potential.

Are you ready to wake up and live your happy ever after?

Like the princess Aurora who was put under a magic spell for one hundred years until love's first kiss awakened her, you are also under a magic spell until you wake up. Are you sleeping or are you aware?

How do you wake up? When you make a conscious decision to change your thinking. This simply means that in the moment you made the decision to change your thoughts your eyes will see the truth. The truth is, you have always had the potential to think and choose in any situation, and any single thought can change the entire direction of your life. Remember, you are a conscious spirit in an earth suit. Your spirit is filled with energy creating infinite possibilities with every thought you focus on. In fact, you are thinking something right now.

Have you ever wondered where your thoughts come from? Don't they often seem so random?

Walt and Aristotle both agree, and Bruce Lipton's current research proves your thoughts are formed from memories, not future events. Yes, it's true, everything you have always wanted already exists in your mind. You came to earth with a purpose. You can experience a new way of thinking, but all thoughts already exist. It's your job to think and choose. Sleeping Beauty sang about this in the song "Once upon a Dream": "I know you, I walked with you, once upon a dream." This phenomenon of believing before you see is a sign that you are awake and in alignment with the higher Truth at work in you. Your visions will appear as if by magic.

If thoughts are things and things are energy, what are you thinking right now?

So many of the world's greatest thinkers agree thoughts are energy. Even Albert Einstein said, "Match the frequency of the reality you want, and you cannot help but get the reality! It can be no other way. This is not philosophy. This is physics." As if it was crazy to think any other way.

Your thoughts hold creative energy, and energy is always vibrating. The way you think and how you feel produces a ripple effect around you. Have you ever thrown a stone in a lake and noticed that one stone produces a ripple effect that is magnified by the surrounding water? This happens with good and bad thoughts. The quality of the vibration is attracting what you are thinking to you like a magnet. Your thoughts also have feeling attached. The quality of the feeling affects the frequency of the vibration. This is all happening in real time. The subconscious can't tell the difference if the thought is happening now or in the past. The real witches and demons of this world, the real magic, all come from the unseen first. It is the meaning you give a thought that determines what you create. How can we fight the monsters under the bed or understand that the dark parts of this world aren't real? You make fear real with your imagination. Think about the last time you were very afraid or anxious. Was what you were thinking actually happening or was it a mere figment of your imagination? Your mind is so powerful that you can actually produce physical symptoms just by thinking about something.

Thankfully this works both ways. Thankfully it is all a choice.

Isn't it true that we are so much more afraid of just how powerful we can be than we are afraid of what we go up against? The stories that you have created keep you from being your 100 percent best version. In order to protect yourself, you make excuses.

Let's circle back and dive a little deeper into the question, where do thoughts come from?

The science of quantum physics has helped to clarify how our thoughts create things. You should now have begun to understand that everything that exists begins with a thought. Thoughts can be positive or negative depending on the feeling you associate with it. For example, when you become aware that you don't have something you want, you will naturally feel like something is missing from your life. This is how you begin creating your circumstances with your imagination. The more

you think about the things you are lacking, the
more you will find lack in your life. However this
also works in reverse. The more you imagine what
it would be like to have the things you desire, the
more your brain naturally starts creating that. Your
brain will use pictures and images of what your
future could look like. This is how successful people
think.

There is a neurological process that begins in the
frontal lobe of your brain. When this creative center
switches on, it begins to send signals to the rest of
your brain. As you chose new images to focus on,
your brain begins firing in new sequences, patterns,
and combinations.

Honestly, most people have thought negative for
so long they don't know how to think any other
way. I have noticed on my own journey that there
are two things that negative-thinking people have in
common. Love was withheld either as a child or as
an adult and destructive criticism could be found in
the past or present.

Both of these are real; however, to choose a new
way of thinking, it's important to identify if either of
these are a cause. If this is true for you, the only way
to rewire is to choose to forgive and move forward
in love. Only replacing negative thoughts with love
can undo the damage this thinking has caused.
There is nothing to "fix" except your thinking.
There is no right or wrong in this life, only choices to
bring you closer to your purpose. In many spiritual

traditions it is taught that you were not created to do this life alone. You are never alone. You were designed for unity. As you open your mind to where the spirit of Truth exists you will become aware of the most intimate connection between God, spirit and man. This is the mystery....has already been decided by Grace before you were born. Remember, you are never alone and the world needs you. God, consciousness, and man are all connected as one living body. This is the mystery that has puzzled scholars for centuries. It is no longer a mystery. Walt knew this too in his attempt to create a world of wonder. When you begin to change your thinking, a higher power within you and all around you begins to manifest and guide you for your highest good. All you dream of and all you desire has already been created in the mind. Remember, you are never alone.

1. List five limiting words you have said about yourself this week.

2. Replace these words with magical words that you can add to your vocabulary

3. What is your earliest childhood memory? How has it made an impact on where you are today?

4. What or who's voice have you been listening to?

5. List five words successful people think about.

CHAPTER 3
SECOND, BELIEVE!

"If you can believe it, you can achieve it."

–Walt Disney

D o you believe you can create a magical life?
I don't mean with spells and witch craft.
When I say the words "magical life," this is not
hocus-pocus. I will not teach you how to cast spells,
but you will learn that self-talk and the use of words
that form your beliefs also create your reality. What
you say you believe and what you truly believe in
your heart are often opposing thoughts. That's the
challenge. The reality is your world is not as real as
you think. Your world is based on your perception,
how you describe it. The way you see something
is based on your beliefs—if you believe it to be so,
then so it is. Each of us sees the world from our own

perspective, so how you describe your magical life is very different from mine.

Nothing happens by accident! Everything that has happened and will happen in your life is completely up to you. Quantum physics proposes that *seeing* is not believing; rather, what you *believe* is what you will see. This will not come from your thoughts and words alone; it will manifest through your actions. What Walt knew is that what you believe about yourself and what you believe is possible will create your reality. Thinking is one thing, but what you really believe is another layer to peel back. This is the difference between a wish and a belief. What you really believe in life is what you really get.

Your mind has a built-in filter system called the RAS, the reticular activating system. Basically, we have so much information to process in any given moment you would be overwhelmed if your mind didn't sort it for you. This filter gives meaning to a thought that is based entirely on what you have learned to believe. This is all happening at a subconscious level. However, what Walt knew is that you can override the RAS with your imagination and choose to believe what you want! This will take a conscious effort on your part.

You are master of your own fate, and each day you can chose to begin a new dream. Like Alice reminds us in the Disney classic *Alice in Wonderland*, "Nothing is impossible when you believe it to be possible"—

If it's as easy as believing, what if every day could be magical?

As a child you had a perfect mind and no limited beliefs until you learned how to worry and doubt yourself. These are not natural instincts. If you are willing to think back and remember when you were a child, you believed in something bigger than yourself. When you become aware of that, something magical will occur. You will be given the key that unlocks that space where dreams are made. You just have to open the door.

Key#2 Believe you already have what you desire, and it appears like magic.

First, you will need to release old beliefs that no longer serve you.

Close your eyes, take a few deep breaths, and allow any limiting beliefs that have stopped you in the past to come into your awareness. Just notice. Don't attach any meaning. The power is in the awareness. Using what you now know about imagination, recreate what you really want to believe by choosing. Replace each negative belief with a new empowering one.

Take a moment to make a list of what came up for you in this space below. As you begin identifying negative beliefs, replace each one with a new truth. For example, if you often feel you are not good enough, you could replace that belief with a statement like "I am more than enough and divinely guided." You will be amazed at how quickly things start to change with a simple shift in what you believe.

What was your favorite Disney classic? Did you have a favorite character? Often, as adults we tend to recreate those characters in real life.

If I were to guess, today you are attracting circumstances that in some way remind you that you are that character. For example, are you playing the victim, hero, or princess? Maybe you are a little mischievous like Peter Pan and never grew up? Maybe you relate to the hero and are always saving people. The point is this: as a child you chose that role. Everything in your personal reality today has been chosen by you. Here's the good news! You can write a new story. You can choose a new character. You can recreate your life. It's a process that's not always easy. There will be people around you that don't understand this new you. You may even lose some friends, but change is always worth the effort.

In recreating my own life I found great courage in the words of Dr. Joe Dispenza:

> When you do decide to make these different choices, don't try to explain yourself to others. Just understand that everyone has to make choices for themselves, including

you. By doing this properly, you will show
up to *yourself* in an unpredictable way. The
beautiful thing about this is that it gives the
people in your life permission to do the same,
and this is, in fact, is one of your greatest
gifts to them.

As you go through the change process, there will
be periods of time when it seems like nothing is
really happening. That's the biological death of the
old self taking place. And it will go down fighting!
But if you consistently do the work every day, your
efforts will become instrumental in unfolding your
new personal reality—and what you'll find is that
it's always worth the effort.

As you continue to read these pages, you and I
are going shift your regular thinking and set sail
with a new perspective. Your eyes are wide open
now, and both feet are on Captain Hook's ship.
Together, we are beginning a new adventure that
will change the way you use your imagination.
Believe me or not, you are using your imagination
right now creating the situation you are in. Your
story is 100 percent based on what you believe. So
why not believe something fabulous?

In this chapter I will share in detail what Walt
knew about the importance of believing in yourself
and your dreams from the wisdom found in the
classic *Snow White*.

> *"Someday my prince will come*
> *Someday I'll find my love*
> *And how thrilling that moment will be*
> *When the prince of my dreams comes to me."*
> —Snow White

Do you feel like life is one big practical joke and that your someday will never arrive?

Most of us are moving day to day, dealing with one thing after another. Does it feel like you just can't break through? The quality of your life is the product of what you are believing in your heart. Life is a mirror. For this reason the prophets of old taught to guard your heart at all cost, for out of it come the troubles of this world. Your outward circumstances are a reflection of what you are believing on the inside. These beliefs are coming to life for you every day. Do you recognize this? Maybe you have been shrugging it off as bad luck. Maybe you believe you deserve the life you are in. You are not alone. Most successful people have struggled to overcome feelings of unworthiness. This one belief about what you deserve will change your whole reality. It's simple. Just as you identified your limiting beliefs, you must now choose. Refuse to believe the lies and choose to replace them with the truth. The truth is, you were born to succeed, and you are divinely guided in that path. Walt was a firm believer in divine intervention. Are you?

My biggest challenge I had to overcome to create my magical life was self-doubt. I struggled for many years feeling unworthy. I was raised in a legalistic religion and taught that God loves me but allows bad things to happen for our own good. I was also taught that He blesses some but not everyone. This is just one example of the limiting beliefs I had to apply truth to. I personally choose not to believe any of that anymore. I believe life is a journey of challenges that we are fully equipped for by a loving God and empowered to overcome. The truth is, you have been given power, and the freedom to choose what you want to believe. God is not the enemy. Lies you choose to believe are the real enemy.

The moment you become aware of this truth, transformation occurs in the twinkle of an eye. There are many examples hidden in Disney classics but the best example of this is Cinderella's transformation. You may be thinking, the transformation was getting the prince, right? Not quite. That was the end result of the choice she made that set her up to win. Her transformation occurred the moment she received the invitation to the ball. Cinderella made a choice to believe she was worthy to receive the invitation without hesitation or doubt. This is how life works. There are endless amounts of possibilities that can happen for you at any moment. If you don't feel worthy to receive them, you will miss them. In fact, you won't even notice them.

Maybe fairytales aren't so make-believe after all.

So, let's talk about you and where you are right now.

Take a minute now to look in the mirror. Really look at yourself. If the evil step mother can ask, so can you! Ask that hidden part of you that knows what you really want. Mirror, mirror on the wall, who do you see? Can you see past your physical body and into the eyes of your future self? Walt knew that who you see is who you are being, and to believe is who you will become. I am—what?

An effective exercise I have used on several occasions is to write a letter to your future self. With great detail describe what you desire as if it's already done. Feel yourself into what this will be like with all the emotion you can. Create your state and watch the magic happen.

Dear future self:

_____

_____

_____

_____

_____

_____

_____

_____

If you are old enough to remember the saying "you have yourself worked up into a state" you will understand this concept. You get yourself into "states," and these states attract similar states to you. You create a state by the things you believe about yourself. It's not even what you say because we say things every day. However, if you say the same thing over and over, eventually you will believe your own words and make them true. Another great thinker, Neville Goddard, describes a state like this.

> *A state is an attitude of mind, a state of experience with a body of beliefs which you live by. Always expressing a state, you identify yourself with it by saying: "I am poor or I am rich. I am known or I am unknown. I am wanted or I am unwanted.*
>
> —Neville Goddard

In the classic Snow White, the seven dwarves are examples of states. Doc, Grumpy, Happy, Sleepy, Bashful, Sneezy, and Dopey are examples of how we can get into habits that become our identity. How often have you identified yourself with one of these states? When you refer to yourself as something, you begin to show up in the world and attract situations to prove yourself right. Soon you have become exactly what you believe. Day after day the dwarves wake up and go to bed living out who they believe they are. Your state of mind determines your outward reality, and your attitude is creating the state you are in.

When you look at a given state with a quantum view of consciousness, you are continuously choosing a possibility based on what you are sensing in your environment. How you are feeling, the thoughts that are forming, and what your gut instinct is saying determine your state. Individually or in combination, these beliefs that have become habits are creating the state of who you are being day to day.

Who have you been showing up as in your life to this point? Is it serving you, or is it time to change your state?

_____

_____

_____

_____

_____

_____

_____

_____

_____

_____

_____

Write down five things you believe to be true about yourself. Then make another list and write five things others often say about you.

_____

_____

_____

_____

_____

_____

_____

_____

_____

_____

_____

_____

_____

_____

_____

_____

_____

_____

_____

_____

Can you see how the beliefs that have created your current state are affecting how others see you as well? If you don't like the state you are in, change it.

How do you get out of a state?

Change what you believe! You must be willing to accept this truth in order to create new states of being. Start acting the way you want to be even if it feels uncomfortable at first. I used to think I was shy, I played small so people wouldn't notice me. In fact, other people confirmed what I was believing and labeled me shy. I realized this state was holding me back from my highest potential. I decided I wanted more for myself and took on a new state. In my new state I consciously chose to believe I was a global influence. I spoke the words even when I didn't believe them. I continued to show up as who I wanted to become, doing the uncomfortable things. This choice created a new state. I began to show up fearful around travel. This is normal when you are stretching yourself. With every new belief you must overcome the old. For weeks prior to leaving on a trip I would begin to feel panic, and fearful thoughts would race through my mind. Many times I would get to the gate and wait until the very last minute to board. I knew I was working myself into a state that was not serving my dreams. In these moments you must chose to fight through the feelings and stay focused on your desired state. It was not easy, but with every win I was one trip closer to being in a state of global influence. Today I travel worldwide leading teams of entrepreneurs. I love teaching them how to win at life. By choosing the desired state that reinforces the life you want, you start to see small wins that lead to big wins.

Are you winning at life? If not, you must create your state to match what you want. Ask yourself this question daily: "What does a winner do?" Then do that! For example, a winning personality uses words like *winning* and *successful*. What about words like *contribution*? Do you believe that you can make a positive impact on someone else's life? Your contribution matters in business and in creating an incredible life, not just for others, but for you and for your family. The state you are in not only affects you, it impacts those around you. When you win, it gives the people around you permission to believe they can win in their own lives.

What drives you to win? Significance or Service? The value you put on either of these will make a huge difference in the life you will experience. Significance is a worthy goal if you are not striving just for the applause. It will eventually bring pain and dissapointment. Service driven significance is rewarding to your soul and empowers those around you. A life of service to others is a life God rewards.

What is your desired state?

I am . . .
List below words that would
describe yourself in your desired state.

_____

_____

_____

_____

Once you have identified your current state,
notice what beliefs are not aligned with your
desired state. Any thoughts or words you use to
describe yourself that do not serve your highest
good must be replaced. Give your state a new
meaning. Ignore any other state but the chosen one.
Focus only on what you want.

Think about Snow White! She was in a state of
innocence and bliss and totally unaware that she
had an enemy trying to steal her heart. Walt knew
that the hidden meaning in her famous name. Snow
White represents your higher self, the highest power
of pure love that exists in each of you to overcome
the world. Snow White was safe in her own reality
because her heart did not deceive her. She remained
in her state of unconditional love and did not
waver in her beliefs. More than what you think
in your mind, it's what you believe in your heart
that determines your state. The heart and mind
connection is powerful. Researcher Gregg Braden
describes it as a conversation:

In each moment of every day, a conversation is taking place inside us. Without a doubt, it's one of the most vital communications we will ever find ourselves engaged in. It's the silent, often subconscious, and never-ending conversation of emotion-based signals between our hearts and our brains, also known as the heart brain connection.

When your heart is pure, it impacts the way you process the meaning of your thoughts. The emotion you attach creates a level of inevitability. The heart is connected to the emotion that you experience as a feeling, which sends signals to your brain. This heart-brain connection is what ultimately creates your state. Thousands of thoughts come and go, but when you attach a feeling with strong emotion to a thought, you have now created a state activated by the heart-brain connection.

Think about the last time you had a thought that caused an emotional reaction? What did it feel like in your body?

The dark forest that Snow White was lost in is a great example of how you may feel when your heart is troubled or confused. Have you ever felt gloomy or even isolated? Sometimes it's hard to see through the trees, especially when it's dark and scary. Often times feeling fear can overtake you if you let it. Your heart beats faster, palms begin to sweat, and negative thoughts can overwhelm you. Before long, you have worked yourself into a fearful state by using your imagination in a self-defeating way. Notice next time you have an emotional reaction. What came first, the feeling or the thought? The evil stepmother appears in many Disney classics and is meant to represent feelings of jealousy, vanity, and revenge. These are thoughts that have high emotion attached. These feelings can create strong deep-rooted beliefs. Holding on to these negative feelings will take you into a state that is destructive.

The apple represents the illusions of this world. Illusions will often be disguised as something we think we want, like the shiny red apple. Temptation and evil don't always come in the form a giant dragon or a recognizable problem. Sometimes it is something as simple as a poisonous thought that really isn't true. We know from the latest research in neuroscience that neuropathways in your brain are being built with every thought—good and bad. These pathways are stored in the RAS that hold memories. It is the feeling you associate with the memory that triggers the emotional reaction. These heart-brain emotional reactions affect your behavior and define what you continue to believe. Think about how you feel most of the day. Those feelings are creating a subconscious state. If a negative state continues to grow over time, you will start to believe that life is just unfair.

You can pretend to be something or someone to those around you, but who *you* believe you are is what you have become.

You are creating yourself! The good news is, you get to choose in any moment to be anything you want. Doing this inner work is so worth it. When you continue to align what you believe and how you show up each day, you get to choose what you want to believe. As you become more aware of the power to choose your state, others will start to notice too. I am no longer labeled shy. I am known as the courageous one that travels all over the world inspiring others to live out their dreams. Those close to you will begin to notice your transformation. Become aware of what people say about you. You may notice you are believing what others say even more than your own words. Listen to what those close to you say about you. This will be the proof that your state has changed. You will also begin to notice others states and can use your words to bring out their highest potential. When I am coaching, I imagine far beyond any limiting beliefs the client can see. I see endless possibilities in everyone. This is greatest gift you can give yourself. When you can see unlimited potential in another, you have mastered the ability to believe in yourself.

1. What did you want to be when you grew up?

2. Who told you that it's not OK to dream big?

3. Grab a mirror and Right five words that describe you.

4. What are 3 habits you consistently do everyday?

5. Name 3 new habits you would like to create your state.

CHAPTER 4
THIRD, DREAM!

.

"A dream is a wish your heart makes,
when you are fast asleep."

—Cinderella

Cinderella said it, but Peter Pan proved it!
Something magical happens when you make
a wish before you go to bed. Not just any kind of
wish though, a specific intention. Walt knew that
this wakeful state right before you fall asleep is
what neuroscientists call lucid dreaming. This is
the time that your subconscious can be accessed to
plant your dreams and wishes. It is similar to that
magical hypnotic state you were in as a child during
your most impressionable years.

"But, Peter, how do we get to Neverland?"
Wendy asked.

Neverland is dreamland, the resting place in your brain you can only access during deep mediation or sleep.

How do you get there? Peter's childlike response was, "Why fly, of course!"

What if it is that easy? What dreams would be possible if you could get to that place?

Peter Pan gives us the answer.

All you have to do is "think of a wonderful thought!" Set your intention and state your desire. The spiritual lesson in this is, to make your dreams a reality you must discipline yourself to think on things that are true and kind and lovely, especially before you go to bed. Never go to bed angry!

I'm sure by now you have recalled those famous words of Peter Pan, which are followed by "all it takes is faith, trust, and pixie dust!"

 Key#3 Magical thinking is to see the world like a child.

Tinkerbell sprinkled the pixie dust, but this is not what gave Peter Pan the "edge" that successful people seem to have. So what was it? It's even more than Peter's childlike faith. It's a habitual way of thinking to maintain a sense of awe in every circumstance. Peter had a sense of wonder about everything, more than just a positive attitude. He viewed life as one big adventure and never wanted to grow up. Most adults hold the belief that we need to "grow up" to get what we want. This could not be further from the truth. A programmed brain is not creative; it can only process old meanings.

How do you "see" the world?

Do you view it with childlike wonder as Peter Pan did? Can you picture your favorite things? Peter tells you, "It's the same as having wings." How you chose to see the world will determine if you can fly. Or have you grown bitter and cynical as an adult like Captain Hook, who was tainted by his circumstances? Did you ever notice that Captain Hook was the only adult in Neverland? He was also the victim, trapped in his own misery caused by his need for revenge. In order to be filled with childlike wonder with an eye for adventure like Peter Pan, any negative adult thinking must be replaced with adventure and awe.

List a few of your favorite things.
It's the same as having wings!

_____

_____

_____

_____

_____

_____

_____

What if I told you that pixie dust is a real thing? It's not the official name, but the concept is accurate. Pixie dust is what powers your imagination. This shouldn't be a shock, given the content of the past chapters. If you could observe pixie dust under a microscope you would see moving quantum particles of light. The swirls of pixie dust that Tinkerbelle sprinkled are actual particles of light, photons that exist in waves and particles at the same time. This is also known as Einstein's theory of light. These waves hold endless possibilities, but they need a human imagination to manifest into reality. Walt knew that pixie dust is the catalyst your imagination needs to manifest dreams into reality. He also knew that the key to unlock the pixie dust is your faith. The power is trusting in your ability to use your imagination and hold unwavering conviction that the dream will come true with faith, trust, and a little pixie dust.

Could Walt have known the mystery of Einstein's quantum particles? Did he really comprehend that by adding pixie dust to your dream was the secret ingredient to manifest it into reality? Peter Pan knew for sure!

If two of the most brilliant minds in history agree, imagination requires a new way of thinking! Who am I to argue?

I was skeptical at first, fighting my own view of the world, which was based on past disappointments. Giving up this way of thinking is not natural. As you grow older life happens, and magical thinking fades away. But what if Walt was right? If you really believed that you could create all your dreams using just your imagination, would you? You can! The ability to dream and apply the science behind pixie dust is always there! It was there from the beginning of creation and will be as long life exists on our planet.

The million-dollar question then is, how do we use this endless amount of pixie dust—particles to create something—right here, right now? Pixie dust exists in the unseen world as waves of possibility in the form of photons, or light particles. In order to form our material world there must be a collapse of these waves, which requires an action on your part. First, you chose an idea to believe in. Focus on what you want and claim it with your words and by your daily action. Create your own story using vivid pictures and all of your senses. These are the magic ingredients needed to turn a dream into reality.

You are a very important part of this equation because nothing can be created without you as the observer. Particles stay in a wave until you put focused attention on them. According to quantum theory, you are made of 99 percent nothing, or I prefer to think of it, as endless possibilities. Until you notice and focus your attention on something, it does not exist. Your dream will stay unseen until you first clearly see it in your mind. Clarity is key. This focused attention is called the observer effect I shared in the previous chapter. You are the observer.

This is why dream boards are so powerful. Do you have a dream board?

Dream boards are key because they are visual! My whole family has their own dream board. I also love to journal my dreams. I write stories of how I want my story to unfold. I have pages of evidence that focused attention works. These pages are filled with dreams written years before they manifested into my reality. How can this be? You *must* observe it before you can create it. There is a universal system working in mankind that allows you to think, speak, observe, and create.

Once you know what you want and can see it clearly, hold your attention on it. It will become a reality. It's the law.

You may be thinking, if it's this easy, why don't I already have everything I dream of? Each of the keys unlocks a system. They can work to some degree separately, but when all four are applied together the chance of creating what you want increases. A great example of this is dreaming of something you want but not believing you can have it. Or thinking about something you want but not giving it attention. I remember travelling with a good friend a few years back in Chicago. My friend was very successful in business and could afford to shop at any of the designer stores. We stopped by a famous brand store of women's handbags. I'll

never forget: she found a handbag and fell in love.
She told me "I have always dreamed of owning one
of these bags." In my mind I was thinking, you
can clearly afford one; why don't you have it? She
had only applied one key. She had a dream, and
it stopped there. She held a limiting belief that
stopped her from creating this dream for herself.
Her thinking was not aligned with her dream.
Memories from her past were stealing her dreams
of the future. This type of thinking and old beliefs
that she was still holding on to are not just about
a handbag. This thinking was also holding her back
from breaking through to more in her business and
relationships. I could see the "child at Christmas"
look in her eyes. She was ready to transform her
thinking. I simply helped her become aware that
she was worthy to have anything she wanted. She
bought that handbag, and her income doubled the
next month! She walked in the store dreaming what
it would be like and walked out with the bag in her
hands. This is powerful.

Why is this important?

The keys work individually to unlock small
dreams, but you didn't buy this book for that. You
have big dreams. To dream *big* requires all four keys
and an unlimited mindset.

Money is a mindset. Happiness is a mindset.
Success in all forms is a mindset.

Dr. Caroline Leaf, a very intuitive mentor,
described it like this:

A mindset is an attitude, or a cluster of thoughts with attached information and emotions that generate a particular perception. They shape how you see and interact with the world. They can catapult you forward, allowing you to achieve your dreams, or put you in reverse drive if you are not careful.—

This is why you must dream like a child. A child's mindset is one that can dream and think without fear and doubt. Children think that anything is possible. Do you remember believing you could fly, travel to the moon, or be the president? Children have a way of verbalizing fearlessly to anyone and everyone about their grand dreams. Guess what? They don't care if you believe them or not. The challenge as an adult is, as you grow up your dreams begin to shrink. Or maybe you hide them for fear of disappointment and fear of what others would say if you shared your dream.

Do you speak your dreams out loud?

Walt knew the power of speaking your dream into reality. Words are magic. Like Abracadabra! Sound familiar? You guessed it, the famous words in Disney movie *Aladdin*. Do you know the actual Hebrew meaning of abracadabra? There is a spiritual connection made thousands of years ago that proves the power behind using words to create.

"I create by speaking; I speak a blessing into physical existence, being derived either from the

Hebrew words '*ab*' (father), '*ben*' (son), and '*ruach hakodesh*' (Holy Spirit), or from the Aramaic '*avra kadavra*,' meaning 'it will be created in my words.'" This is a profound hidden message Walt knew. You get to choose your words for good or evil. This is when surrendering your imagination to truth is critical. Most people think and speak words based on past experience. This type of thinking comes from old patterns not nessisarily truth. The truth is your thoughts are not your own. They come from outside forces. Words can be twisted to mean different things that result in a totally different outcome based on truth or lies. The more you discipline yourself to walk in truth the easier it is to chose words that create for you and not against you.... When words are used in the right context they create dreams where as in the wrong context can lead to nightmares.

This truth also aligns with quantum physics. Fast forward to the 21st century: we have solid evidence based research that proves your words are energy that form vibrations!

In fact, everything has a vibration. Your dream is a vibration. Match that vibration to who you are being and what you are speaking, and it will quickly appear. Think back to high school chemistry class. Do you remember learning about atoms, and that everything is made up of atoms? These atoms are in a constant state of motion, and depending on the speed of these atoms, things can appear as a solid, liquid, or gas. Sound is a vibration, and so are thoughts. Everything that manifests itself in your life is there because it matches your vibration. You are a walking magnet. In order for your dream to become a reality, the dream must be in alignment with your vibration. Like attracts like.

How can you change your vibration to match your dream?

To get to the end of the story you want to create, you first need to go back to the beginning. Why? You now know that thoughts become things, but what you may not know is that every thought you have today is based on a past memory. Like the story of my friend and the designer handbag, these thoughts from your past trigger feelings, and it's these feelings that make up the vibration. When you are thinking about your dream, can you feel the butterflies in your tummy or do have a feeling of dread? You are choosing what comes next by how you feel when you imagine your dream. Think back to when you were a child. Many of you as kids played in blanket forts or tents, letting your childhood imagination run and play. Some of you may not have such pleasant memories. Some of you are "living the dream" while others may be living a nightmare. All of these memories are important and have brought you exactly where you are right now. You have been dreaming your entire life unaware of how things get created, until now.

Have you ever been around a very successful person? Don't you agree they have a certain vibe about them? What about someone not so fortunate—can you feel a different energy around them?

1. How do you feel right now?

_____

_____

_____

_____

_____

2. List three feelings that come up when you imagine your dream.

_____

_____

_____

_____

_____

3. Do those feelings match how you would feel if your dream was already a reality?

_____

_____

_____

_____

4. List three feelings you will experience when your
   dream comes true.

---

5. How can you change your vibration to match
   your dream?

Just writing this you felt a shift in your mindset.
Hold on to those positive feelings every time you
imagine your dream. Dreaming is an art! It takes
some practice, but in time you will become an
imagination master.

The ability to transform dreams into reality
won't happen overnight. I was fortunate to
become very aware of dreaming at a young age.
I was blessed to have been raised in a safe and
loving home with plenty of opportunities to use
my imagination. I remember an old table in the

dining room with the tattered rug underneath.
I was only four years old, so I fit just nicely. I
imagined this space as my own secret castle. In
the living room there was an old record player.
I remember the lid was quite heavy for my tiny
four-year-old hands, and the records seemed so
delicate. I would run my fingers across the grooves
as I placed it on the player and allowed the arm
to land so carefully. I wondered in my tiny little
mind, How did these magical lines create this
music and bring stories to life? Most kids that age
wouldn't care, but I did. I wanted to know how
the world worked. My music box baffled me the
same way. I've always been one to question how
things work, and I still do today.

Although I grew up in a two-parent home,
they were often unavailable. Like most parents
of that generation they were busy building a life
and supporting a family. I didn't mind being
alone, though, because I had my secret castle.
I had princesses, wizards, and elves as friends.
I flew with Peter Pan and traveled to far-off
places and magical lands, all before first grade.
It was here under that dining table that I first
learned the power of imagination. I formed my
belief system that anything is possible. My
neuropathways were lined with gold streets
and fairy godmothers. I was fully convinced by
Cinderella that dreams do come true. Cinderella
sang in the Disney's movie, "A Dream Is a Wish

Your Heart Makes." I believed her then, and I still believe.

Your dream is also your story that you live each day.

Minute by minute you are creating your own adventure! Why not make it a great one?

CHAPTER 5
AND LAST . . . DARE!

"It's kinda fun to do the impossible."

—Walt Disney

The key word is "do" and the vehicle is you. You are riding the wave of possibilities in your mind every second that you are conscious. Your mind is like a magic carpet. The fun part is, you get to choose where it will take you.

If you Dare!

Key#4 Dare to take action and jump on the magic carpet.

The power of your imagination can help you accomplish all of your dreams, but nothing can happen until you take action.

When you think about the magic carpet in the Disney classic Aladdin, it moves like waves of quantum particles. The photons I refer to as pixie dust are both wave and particle at the same time. Your vehicle to create your dreams is essentially like a magic carpet. Imagine your thoughts and visions as wavelike, with unlimited potential of swirling energy. This energy fills the supernatural spaces we can't see with human eyes. Science calls this space the quantum field of possibility. It is a space filled with pixie dust waiting for you to make a choice. The first step in any journey is to choose Decide what direction you are going and take action Say yes and jump on your magic carpet. Daring to take action is the key. Easy to say, but I get it. Some of you have been feeling stuck for a long time.

Have you ever felt empty or spinning, unable to choose a direction? If so, you are not in a creative space. You must take action to collapse the waves. When a wave that was spinning in supernatural space collapses, quantum physics describes this phenomena as the possibility becoming actuality. Now is the time to move forward boldly, and take action. Decide. Make a choice to move your dream out of the unseen space and into your reality.

Napoleon Hill called this "defiantness of purpose."

Get clear about what you want and where you want to go. It's not always easy, but it sure is fun. When you are riding the magic carpet of life, the journey isn't always smooth. Walt knew to focus on the journey. How many times did he fail only to jump back on his magic carpet and ride another wave? The secret is surrendering to the higher Truth that fills the space we can't see. God moves the waves. Trust that if you were given a dream you have everything you need to see it through. This can be a struggle.

How many times have you tried to take the wheel? You know where you're headed and have it all mapped out, then bam! Road work. Need to switch direction. Do you get anxious about this, or can you learn to trust that the magic carpet will take you exactly where you need to be at the exact right time? Can you imagine a long journey where every other day you tell the pilot to take a different direction or stop while you think about whether you should go on? You would never arrive at the final destination. Your magic carpet only knows one speed: *go*!

A magic carpet has no brakes, no steering wheel, no seatbelt, no handlebars. It just goes where you tell it to with ease. The trick is to sit relaxed and not resist its movement. If you try to steer it, you may fall off course. How often have you tried to force your dream to happen? This is called resistance. You cause resistance when you worry about the how, where, and when. Learning to become nonresistant can help you in your journey. Life is magical when you learn to sit back, relax, and enjoy your magic carpet ride.

We are nearing the end of our journey together and I wonder, does all of this sound like science fiction? A bunch of woo woo and hocus pocus rather than a self-help book? Quantum physics can certainly sound like science fiction. The reality is that one hundred years ago so did airplanes, computers, and cell phones. The human race is advancing to new levels of awareness. You may be thinking all the quantum talk is a little more like science fiction than self-help but the amazing thing about science is that once you know the equations, you can manipulate them to work in different ways. If you are not growing in your thinking you are shrinking!

Just like imagination! You must become a magician and scientist and realize you are divine all in one if you are planning on creating something from nothing. Manifesting dreams does require all these skills and more. It takes focus, attention, and setting goals. However, it also requires a letting go, preferably while having fun and enjoying life.

Relax into it!

Amit Goswami, a brilliant professor and quantum physicist, made this statement that describes how so often we think we know best.

After much research into many case histories, researchers found that something different was going on. Scientist would work very hard to solve a problem. They would find some answers—some hints. And then they would just relax. Do nothing. And often the breakthrough ideas spring forth from that relaxed state.–

Dr. Goswami calls it the "do-be-do-be-do."

This reminds me of the fairy godmother's famous magic words in the classic *Cinderella*—"Bippity boppity BOO!

Every dream begins with a wish.

Maybe you want a million dollars? Maybe your dream is to be a mother? Everyone's dream is different, but the keys to create it are the same.

Cinderella had to take action. She had things to do first in order to be ready for her destiny. Cinderella prepared, yet she was never concerned about the how or when. She stayed focused on her dream of meeting the prince with a positive attitude. Cinderella was in a state of gratitude and love despite her circumstance. She had trust in her good and fully expected to meet Prince Charming. Even Cinderella had a moment of despair, but that did not stop her from achieving her goal.

What circumstance are you in right now that you would dare to change to achieve your dream?

_____

_____

_____

_____

_____

It's often in times of despair we find our greatest strength and courage. If you don't give up your fairy godmother will show up for you as well. She may come in the form of a person or an unexpected turn of events. Rest assured, you are always guided. It could even be you. You may get the opportunity to be a fairy godmother to someone else someday as well.

Just wave your magic wand, right?

I get it. It's not as easy as it sounds, but it really is. You make it difficult when you listen to things outside yourself. Once you learn that you can get those other voices in your head out and into the stillness of your heart, divine inspiration will be your guide. Ask, ask, ask . . .

You can ask all the questions you want with multiple possibilities. We just need to keep an open mind and become "Curiouser, curiouser, and curiouser"—*Alice in Wonderland.*

The one question you do need a very clear answer to before taking any action toward your dream goals is:

What do you *really* want?

Set goals. Set huge goals that seem impossible. Then get very clear on what you really want. The key to create is clarity. Before you take action, It's important to have a clear vision.

Write your *big* vision below, then copy it and keep it in front of you, somewhere so that you see it daily. Where do you see yourself in five years from today?

_____

_____

_____

_____

_____

_____

_____

_____

_____

_____

_____

_____

_____

_____

_____

_____

_____

_____

_____

_____

Focus is the hocus pocus!

That's the real magic. You always get what you focus on! Not what's happening right now; focus on how you want your story to end. Skip all the details of how and when and just imagine you are already there. By doing this often, your brain will automatically prompt you to take action in the right direction. You will naturally do the things you need to do in order to manifest your desire.

Here is a visualization exercise I do myself once my intention is clear. Hold the desired thought in your mind. Now, picture the thought inside an electron spinning fast, really fast like at the speed of light. See the intention riding the waves of possibility. As you see your desire spinning, feel as if you're already there, declare it with your words, and let it go. Trust the dream is flying through the universe on your magic carpet and has arrived at the destination.

I'll bet Walt knew the truth behind the magic carpet.

Maybe a magic carpet is not your style. What if I gave you the keys to a brand-new Porsche—would you take it for a drive? Well, yeah! But so many of you would let it sit in your driveway, afraid it may be too fast. Some of you don't want to even sit in it in case you scratch it. God forbid I might come to take it back because you think you really don't deserve it.

What stops you from jumping in? From taking massive action toward your dream?

Alice in Wonderland had a problem called indecisiveness or wavering. Do you?

"If I had a world of my own, everything would be nonsense. Nothing would be what it is, because everything would be what it isn't. And contrary wise, what is, it wouldn't be. And what it wouldn't be, it would. You see?"

You may be shaking your head as you read this, but there is so much truth in this quote. Alice was trying to ask us "Why do you take life so seriously?" Stop trying to figure it out. Make a decision and just go for it. The point is, in any given second you can create and are creating exactly what you choose! Any sort of thinking otherwise is an illusion. What you choose, you get. Often times you are not even aware you are making a choice; it subconscious. Even when you waver you choose back and forth. You are choosing to remain stuck. You may make a choice toward your dream and then a choice that takes you backwards. When you feel this happening, this is the time to be more focused on what you want more than ever. This is the time to jump in with both feet.

Wavering is like waves crashing in the ocean. You won't get anywhere rocking back and forth.

So you think you're too busy to dream?

If you are not working toward your own dreams, I can guarantee you are working for someone else's.

"Hurry, hurry, hurry, I'm late, I'm late!!!." — Rabbit. Sound familiar?

Most of us are running on autopilot creating the same circumstances day after day, seldom getting what we really want. Don't be too hard on yourself; society has had a hand in your conditioning. From first grade on you were taught to walk single file, only speak in turn, eat at given times, play at given times, and the list goes on. It doesn't stop there! Do you remember day one of your first job? Clock in and don't be late! The daily grind. This will not change unless you do. You and I must make a conscious decision to step out of the box and dare to dream again.

Begin to take action in the direction of your dream today!

The rabbit is a great example of your daily grind, running in circles late, late, late. We think where we are going is so very important. Someone is expecting you. The truth is we have all the time in the world, exactly the amount we need to fulfill our purpose on time. What is time anyway? Man created time as we understand it. In the supernatural realm there are no deadlines. There are plans for you that were chosen before you were born. Stepping into that destiny can be intimidating when you have been programmed to believe life is just one day after another.

Perhaps you are in a habit of doing things a certain way. Habits can be hard to break when you get in a routine. Just like the seven dwarves. They worked and whistled day in and day out: "Hi

ho hi ho . . .," but nothing ever changed! *Dwarf*
is another way of saying small. Sure they took
action every day but not in the direction of their
dreams. Their thinking and habits kept them small.
Habitual thinking and routine block imagination.
I'm not saying your dream won't take work. This
is not the same as inspired action. This is not what
"dare to dream" looks like.

How are you conducting your daily action? You
are doing something. Is it keeping you small or
allowing you to play *big*?

What does your day look like? Are you going
through the motions or thriving in your job? Are
you living with purpose or are you just surviving?
Winning at work can be thrilling and rewarding,
but if you are noticing self-talk like failure,
boredom, or not good enough, pay attention. You
should love what you do. Is your work something
that draws your focus away from what you really
want? Think about last week and the hours you
put into your business or your job. Did you neglect
things important to you in exchange for work?
Who do you show up as every day in your job,
relationships, and life? If you aren't happy, only
you can change that. You get one life and have the
exact amount of time you need.

What if you could dare to change the meaning
you have attached to time? Time is sold to us
as a precious commodity, something real and
tangible. We've been raised with this idea that

we live along some invisible line from birth to
death. We are taught that time holds some kind
of invaluable currency that we must spend wisely.
We each have the same twenty-four hours a day.
What are you using those hours on? It circles
back to perception. Similarly, is the idea of work,
which is a four letter word if you attach the wrong
meaning. Work is hard, meaningless, repetitive, etc.
. . . all expectations. Where did your expectations
originate? The part of you that tells you where you
must be, what you have to do, what you should
look like. The Rabbit in *Alice in Wonderland* is
anything you chase or that's chasing you. He is the
voice in your head, "You are late!" "You didn't
finish that on time!" "You forgot to call the client!"
"Did you send out that email?" "I'll do it later."

Some of you may have heard about a secret that
you can just think things into reality. It's half true.

Thoughts alone will not bring your dream
to reality, or we would all have what we want.
Thoughts can have you chasing the rabbit in the
wrong direction. The reality is you must dare to
say yes to what you really want. Your willingness
to risk it all for your dream is what will pay off.
Make a conscious effort to get clarity and then take
action to get what you want. Know what you want,
be willing to go after it, and go *all in*.

This will take some deep conversations with
yourself. Let go of all perceptions and judgments

and allow your higher-than-conscious self to guide you. This is the inner work I dare you to do.

Alice called this the rabbit hole.

The rabbit hole is who we are on the inside. When Alice goes down the hole she is searching introspectively. Sometimes you start seeing things that you wouldn't normally see. It seemed like she was seeing things that didn't make sense. But if we take the time to truly understand and practice checking in with yourself daily, you will only get better and better and better. I suggest getting into a relaxed state through prayer or meditation. This allows your brain to rest and can help bring things about yourself into awareness that you have been missing. I practice the art of stillness and silence. Find a quiet comfortable place to lie on your back perfectly still. Try not to make any movement while you breathe slowly and deeply. Become aware that your body is connected to something much bigger than yourself that is guiding you. Listen to your inner voice. This is a good time to speak an affirmation or make a request. Try it for five minutes a day and work yourself up to an hour. Your brain will rewire itself over time as you discover hidden truth about yourself.

It's up to you. How far down do you want to go?

That is the question Alice was asked, how deep she wanted to go. How much are you willing to face and be open to look at those things and heal and to grow? You have to be willing to do the work, to face the unimagined things hiding in our own rabbit hole. Are you ready to go deep?

The rabbit also signifies your ego. In most circles, the ego gets a pretty bad rap. The reason for this is that the ego, to some extent, is the principle in our psyches that separates us from one another. The truth is, in a quantum world everything is consciousness, so no such separation exists. The ego does exist. Sometimes it is depicted as a dark figure or enemy that keeps us from realizing our true potential. Sometimes it is our friend and provides the confidence needed to win. But at its most basic, the ego is simply a tool that helps us organize the various aspects of our personality. It's like a veil that helps you function in the world. The ego is a tool that we use to navigate the world. Sometimes the rabbit is there to protect you, and sometimes it can be detrimental to your success. For example, all self-sabotage is created by the ego. Fear is an illusion that is based on false perception of a future event that hasn't happened yet. Fear prevents you from taking action to pursue the dream you have in your heart.

If you only knew how powerful you really are.

The real question your ego will ask is, why not you?

The answer is inside of you. You just had to ask. Each time you ask a question, you will get the answer. Ask and you will receive that which can't be explained in the natural. There is a place in your subconscious where ego no longer has first say. It is the place where you go inside yourself and deep down the rabbit hole. For some this is not a place you like to go, but if you dare, the answer is always there.

Alice had to enter here to answer her own question: "Who in the world am I?" That is the great puzzle. We all must go through this tunnel to get to our own "wonderland."

Once you dare to go down the rabbit hole, you are in control. You can choose to listen in a different place and a different voice, one that is being divinely guided, and all that noise fades away.

The rabbit hole is a place to discover who you truly are. In your quiet time of being still you travel inward to ask yourself: Who am I?

What do I want?

Where am I going?

Here lies the struggle. Ego is not the enemy. You are your own enemy when you choose thoughts that take you off course. The enemy is in your mind. Thousands of contradicting thoughts have formed your belief system.

"This is impossible."

"Only if you believe it is."

The rabbit can also be your friend guiding you in the right direction. Who will you listen to?

What about that "other" voice you hear when making a decision or a random idea that seems to spring from the air? Has this ever happened to you? If it has, it can be hard to understand. Sometimes when things like this happen, we are quick to dismiss them as weird or imagined. I get it. I did that in the beginning too. But I have learned not to ignore them. I want to encourage you to pay attention, even to the thoughts that seem way out there. The reality is you heard your higher than conscious self guiding you for your highest good. This is not your ego. It is a unique part of you that is spirit. You are connected to a higher Truth that is beyond time and space. Your creator is nudging you from the realm of all possibility.

Have you ever experienced a time in your life where you needed an answer and you heard a voice like a random thought and you wondered where it came from? That is your intuitive self, your spirit. It is the part of you that is aligned with creative consciousness. Haven't you ever wondered whose voice that is? I know you have argued back and forth with this "imaginary" voice. If it's not the rabbit, who is narrating the story of your life? If you seek, you will find that answer.

_____

_____

_____

_____

_____

_____

How do you want your story to unfold?

It isn't just your life story. It's every story. It's every moment with your family, every doctor visit, every business deal. You have the power to write your own story every day of your life. Or will you allow fear, procrastination, or blame to write your story?

Procrastination is a sneaky form of self-sabotage.

I get it. It's hard to be daring when you are afraid of failing. I know you make excuses just like I do when I am afraid to just go for it.

It isn't that you don't know how, or that you don't want to. You are delaying doing what you need to do. I have found that this can be because you have been hanging on to a limiting belief. Some part of you has doubts about your ability to complete the task, so you procrastinate and delay doing it rather than face the outcome of finishing the task. Sometimes people will procrastinate, not just out of fear of failure, but they are actually worried it will be successful. Do you have a fear of success because of the sacrifice and responsibility that come with success? Increased responsibility means more work. Or, it could be fear based out of concern you may disappoint someone. The fear of letting someone important down can cause huge delays in execution. Have you ever used fear as an excuse to stay where you are in an unwanted circumstance?

To dare takes courage.

Is there a magic potion for that? There is not something you can swallow, but there are two things I have found helpful in rewiring your brain to move forward: love and gratitude. Even with these tools in your pocket it takes commitment to dare to go after your dreams. There will be moments when your ego takes over, but I will promise you this:

With love and gratitude you become unstoppable.

We all know it is good to stop and smell the roses every once in a while—to pause and realize how much we have be grateful for. But did you know that gratitude is essential to success? If you can't appreciate what you have to be thankful for right now, it is harder to achieve what you desire in the future.

In fact, gratitude changes the brain and body for the better! Research on the effects gratitude has on our biology shows how being thankful increases our longevity, our ability to use our imagination, and our ability to problem-solve.

Gratitude makes us feel that life is worth living, which brings mental health benefits in a positive feedback loop that leads to more resilience—the ability to bounce back quicker during hard times. Gratitude is therefore essential to overcoming difficult circumstances and achieving success in all areas of your life!
—Dr. Leaf

You get to be grateful. You get to choose love.

What are some ways you can develop a "gratitude mindset"? I have a gratitude journal and make it a priority to write five things I am grateful for each day. This is a great practice to keep your mind from complaining about what you don't have or the circumstance you are in right now.

What are five things you are grateful for right now?

_____

_____

_____

_____

_____

_____

_____

Walt knew there is a hidden message in *Cinderella* about overcoming circumstances with love and gratitude. She was an orphan who had bad circumstances, but she made a choice to remain in a state of love and gratitude. Cinderella did not complain about her situation; it was as if her world was not what she saw on the outside. Cinderella did not hesitate when told she could attend the ball. She never made excuses that she had nothing to wear or too much work to do. Instead she was grateful for her mice friends and the little she had to make her own dress. Then she took massive action.

She not only completed her tasks, she worked
even harder to finish. She remained steadfast and
focused. Cinderella chose to be humble and hungry.
Before her mother died, she taught Cinderella who
she really was—a worthy princess. She taught her to
have courage and be kind. This radiated from her,
and although she may not have felt worthy because
of her situation, she chose to remain humble and
kind. Humility is a form of gratitude and a great
transformer! Cinderella also never complained. It's
hard to complain when you are grateful. How often
do you find yourself complaining about little things?
You can choose to complain and blame others for
your circumstance, or you can be open to see the
truth of how you really got there. Cinderella knew
what she wanted and took action to get to the ball.
She dared to believe it was possible.

Cinderella's state of gratitude attracted the right
circumstance. Her decision to remain in a loving
state through her circumstances brought her the
desire of her heart. The prince fell instantly in love
with her authentic beauty. The more you grow in
love, the more authentic you become.

Love is the most powerful emotion in the
universe. It's why you love Disney classics. Love
is a magnetic force that draws more love to itself.
The more you love yourself and others, the more
you will create things to love. The alternative is
to hate and believe lies. We are bound by love or
lies. If you aren't walking in love, then you are

walking in a belief that love and freedom simply aren't for you. Without love your dream will never become a reality. Life will remain a struggle. In every circumstance you have a choice, to love or to hate. These aren't just choices in life. This isn't a business choice, or a relationship choice.

Love begins with you.

Do you love yourself? I mean the real, authentic you. If not, why not? If you throw away all the keys and take one thing from this book, I urge you to fall in love with you first. That is your "happily ever after." Any big dream you have will be meaningless without love.

We all really just want one thing from life: to love and be loved.

> *"The greatest risk you will ever take is to be seen as you are."*
>
> —Cinderella

You need to know this, and I am right there with you. It's the same reason why world records are continually broken, and why ultra-marathon runners can keep running further and further. It's why scientists keep find smaller and smaller and bigger and bigger stuff. All highly successful people are grateful, just like Cinderella. They know exactly what they want and go after it. Sure, Cinderella had a little help from her fairy godmother, but you are your own fairy godmothers and have unlimited wishes. Your imagination is the magic wand. Every fairytale needs a princess, and every legend needs a hero to love and be loved. That, my friend, is *you*! Yes, you get the lead role to play in your own life. You get to choose each day how you want the story to begin and end. You chose your happily ever after.

The question is, will you dare to take the lead role or settle to watch from the audience?

Why is this important to create the life you want today? Not next year or maybe someday, but right now?

Because "waiting is a waste of time."

Anything you can dream of you can achieve! All possibilities already exist. You have all four keys to unlock the power of your imagination; you just need to dare!

So, why not you?

1. What do you REALLY want?

2. List five people that can encourage and keep you accountable

3. Name three people that have accomplished what you desire. Reach out to these people and ask them for one tip how they did it.

4. What are you willing to sacrifice to reach your dream?

5. What will you dare to do that is out of your comfort zone?

CHAPTER 6
MY WHY

Dear Reader,
    Sometimes we need a little help with our imaginative ability. That is what is called divine inspiration, the aha! moment that shifts you from one reality into another with a quantum leap. Suddenly a thought you gave an unhealthy meaning to is transformed into truth. New representations become your new reality! Before the day I heard "quantum," I was not at all interested in science. I have always been fascinated by how things work and the "but why" hard questions of life. In high school I was a B student at best and frankly did not use that left side of my brain. I also failed chemistry in college so the word quantum made no sense to me. The fact that I now have a PhD in quantum integrative medicine is proof that

perception can change your reality. Any form of science or math concepts went way over my head as they did anyone who was not majoring in them, and it was beyond me to truly want to spend any of my time in that world. I wasn't going to need or use any of that in my life! Little did I know, all the how and why questions I had as a child could be explained by quantum physics, which explains everything about life as we know it. I had given a whole new meaning to the idea of science.

I understand now I had a quantum leap experience. In that split-second moment my connection with consciousness heard the word *quantum* and downloaded things about light particles and concepts that kept great minds like Einstein up at night. How could I know these things when in college science and science theory made my brain hurt? I believe at that moment, I had remembered my assignment to help people understand the connection between science and scripture. My inner and outer world had aligned. I had many deep questions about life. I asked, and the door was opened.

Why are we here?

What's our purpose?

Who is our creator, really?

I had ideas about each of these that began at a young age that I thought were just crazy. When I began my PhD and my professors spoke a language that made total sense to me I knew this information needed to be shared. I used to fear life and death. Now life and even death make absolute sense when quantum physics is applied to bring you clarity and peace. I saw the meaning of life in a new fresh light. The reason quantum physics makes so much sense to me is because it operates outside natural laws. With the beliefs I held since I was a child, operating outside natural laws was already part of my life! Science and scripture have always been entangled; it just took a few hundred years for technology to confirm what our forefathers knew.

The years that followed this moment have been life changing. But first, I had to dare and take action.

I began to dig deeply into quantum physics and the power of our thoughts, which led to my meeting Dr. Caroline Leaf. Dr. Leaf travels the world sharing her work on the study of how our thoughts create our reality and has inspired the scientific community to engage with the possibility of a higher Truth. It was through meeting Dr. Leaf that quantum physics affirmed that science and spirituality align and in combination can help apply the principles to everyday life.

I too applied the principles that I learned about quantum physics in connection to my faith and saw miraculous doors in my life open. I was able to use my imagination and create the life I wanted for me and my family. The best part? You can do it too!

If I had not been open to dare, this awareness that opened a whole new adventure in pursing my PhD and my journey to seeing the world with a quantum view might have never became my reality

What is it that *you* will dare to do?

IMAGINATION MANIFESTO

*"Venture outside
your comfort zone.
The rewards are worth it."*

—Rapunzel (*Tangled*)

_____

_____

_____

_____

_____

_____

_____

_____

_____

_____

_____

_____

_____

*"All it takes
is faith and trust."*

—Peter Pan (*Peter Pan*)

_____

_____

_____

_____

_____

_____

_____

_____

_____

_____

_____

_____

"A little consideration,
a little thought for others,
makes all the difference."

—Eeyore (*Winnie the Pooh*)

_____

_____

_____

_____

_____

_____

_____

_____

_____

_____

_____

*"Even miracles take
a little time."*

—Fairy Godmother (*Cinderella*)

_____

_____

_____

_____

_____

_____

_____

_____

_____

_____

_____

_____

"If you focus on what you left behind, you will never be able to see what lies ahead."

—Gusteau (*Ratatouille*)

_____

_____

_____

_____

_____

_____

_____

_____

_____

_____

_____

_____

_____

"The flower that blooms in adversity is the most rare and beautiful of all."

—The Emperor (*Mulan*)

_____

_____

_____

_____

_____

_____

_____

_____

_____

_____

_____

_____

_____

"You control your destiny—
you don't need magic
to do it. And there are
no magical shortcuts to
solving your problems."

—Merida (*Brave*)

*"A true hero isn't measured
by the size of his strength,
but by the strength
of his heart."*

—Zeus (*Hercules*)

_____

_____

_____

_____

_____

_____

_____

_____

_____

_____

_____

_____

_____

"Don't just fly, soar."

—**Dumbo** (*Dumbo*)

---

*"In every job that must
be done, there is an
element of fun."*

—Mary Poppins (*Mary Poppins*)

"Life's not a spectator sport. If watchin' is all you're gonna do, then you're gonna watch your life go by without ya."

—Laverne (*The Hunchback of Notre Dame*)

_____

_____

_____

_____

_____

_____

_____

_____

_____

_____

_____

_____

_____

"The problem is not the problem. The problem is your attitude *about the problem."*

—Jack Sparrow (*Pirates of the Caribbean*)

_____

_____

_____

_____

_____

_____

_____

_____

_____

_____

_____

_____

_____

*"Believe you can,
then you will."*

—**Mulan** (*Princess Stories*)

_____

_____

_____

_____

_____

_____

_____

_____

_____

_____

_____

_____

"Today is a good day to try."

—**Quasimodo** (*The Hunchback of Notre Dame*)

_____

_____

_____

_____

_____

_____

_____

_____

_____

_____

_____

_____

_____

_____

"If you don't know where you want to go, then it doesn't matter which path you take."

—The Cheshire Cat (*Alice in Wonderland*)

_____

_____

_____

_____

_____

_____

_____

_____

_____

_____

_____

_____

*"The things that make me
different are the things
that make me ME."*

—**Piglet** (*Winnie the Pooh*)

_____

_____

_____

_____

_____

_____

_____

_____

_____

_____

_____

_____

_____

"It's better to use your head than break your back."

—Ernst Robinson (*Swiss Family Robinson*)

_____

_____

_____

_____

_____

_____

_____

_____

_____

_____

_____

_____

_____

"Admit defeat, and defeat will surely admit you into permanent custody."

—Beret Girl (*An Extremely Goofy Movie*)

_____

_____

_____

_____

_____

_____

_____

_____

_____

_____

_____

_____

_____

*"Listen with your heart,
you will understand."*

—Grandmother Willow (*Pocahontas*)

_____

_____

_____

_____

_____

_____

_____

_____

_____

_____

_____

_____

_____

"Your identity is your most valuable possession. Protect it."

—**Elastigirl** (*The Incredibles*)

_____

_____

_____

_____

_____

_____

_____

_____

_____

_____

_____

_____

_____

_____

"Oh yes, the past can hurt.
But the way I see it, you
can either run from it
or learn from it."

—**Rafiki** (*The Lion King*)

_____

_____

_____

_____

_____

_____

_____

_____

_____

_____

_____

_____

"You're braver than you believe, and stronger than you seem, and smarter than you think."

—**Winnie the Pooh** (*Pooh's Most Grand Adventure*)

_____

_____

_____

_____

_____

_____

_____

_____

_____

_____

_____

_____

*"If you don't think,
then you shouldn't talk."*

—**March Hare** (*Alice in Wonderland*)

"Our fate lives within us.
You only have to be brave
enough to see it."

—Merida (*Brave*)

_____

_____

_____

_____

_____

_____

_____

_____

_____

_____

_____

_____

_____

"I'm only brave when I have to be. Being brave doesn't mean you go looking for trouble."

—Mufasa (*The Lion King*)

_____

_____

_____

_____

_____

_____

_____

_____

_____

_____

_____

_____

"Giving up is for rookies."

—Philoctetes (*Hercules*)

_____

_____

_____

_____

_____

_____

_____

_____

_____

_____

_____

_____

_____

_____

"Always let your conscience be your guide."

—The Blue Fairy (*Pinocchio*)

_____

_____

_____

_____

_____

_____

_____

_____

_____

_____

_____

_____

_____

"I give myself very good advice,
but I very seldom follow it."

—**Alice** (*Alice in Wonderland*)

"Happiness is the richest thing we will ever own."

—Donald Duck

_____

_____

_____

_____

_____

_____

_____

_____

_____

_____

_____

_____

_____

"Just because it's what's done, doesn't mean it's what should be done."

—Cinderella (*Cinderella*)

_____

_____

_____

_____

_____

_____

_____

_____

_____

_____

_____

_____

_____

*"Sometimes the right path
is not the easiest one."*

—Grandmother Willow (*Pocahontas*)

_____

_____

_____

_____

_____

_____

_____

_____

_____

_____

_____

_____

_____

"Change is good."

—Rafiki (*The Lion King*)

_____

_____

_____

_____

_____

_____

_____

_____

_____

_____

_____

_____

_____

"The only thing predictable about life is its unpredictability."

—**Remy** (*Ratatouille*)

_____

_____

_____

_____

_____

_____

_____

_____

_____

_____

_____

_____

*"Remember, you're the
one who can fill the
world with sunshine."*

—**Snow White** (*Snow White and
the Seven Dwarves*)

"Do not be followed by its commonplace appearance. Like so many things, it is not what is outside, but what is inside that counts."

—Merchant (*Aladdin*)

_____

_____

_____

_____

_____

_____

_____

_____

_____

_____

_____

_____

_____

"Now, think of the happiest things. It's the same as having wings."

—Peter Pan (*Peter Pan*)

_____

_____

_____

_____

_____

_____

_____

_____

_____

_____

_____

_____

"All our dreams can come true, if we have the courage to pursue them."

—Walt Disney

CONNECT WITH
CARLA BURNS

Imagination Master Cruise

YouTube
drcarlaburnstv.com

Facebook Group
Create Your Magical Life
https://www.facebook.com/
groups/1912137045506881

Instagram
https://www.instagram.com/thecarlaburns

Website
drcarlaburns.com